junk style

Melanie Molesworth

photography by **Tom Leighton**

LONDON • NEW YORK

Senior Designer Larraine Shamwana
Senior Editor Sian Parkhouse
Production Manager Kate Mackillop
Text by Melanie Molesworth and Alice
Westgate

First published in Great Britain in 1998
This edition published in 2013 by
Ryland Peters & Small
20–21 Jockey's Fields
London WC1R 4BW
and
519 Broadway, Fifth Floor
New York, NY 10012
www.rylandpeters.com

10 9 8 7 6 5 4 3 2 1

ISBN 978 1 84975 368 5

A CIP record for this book is available
from the British Library.

Printed in China

junk style

contents

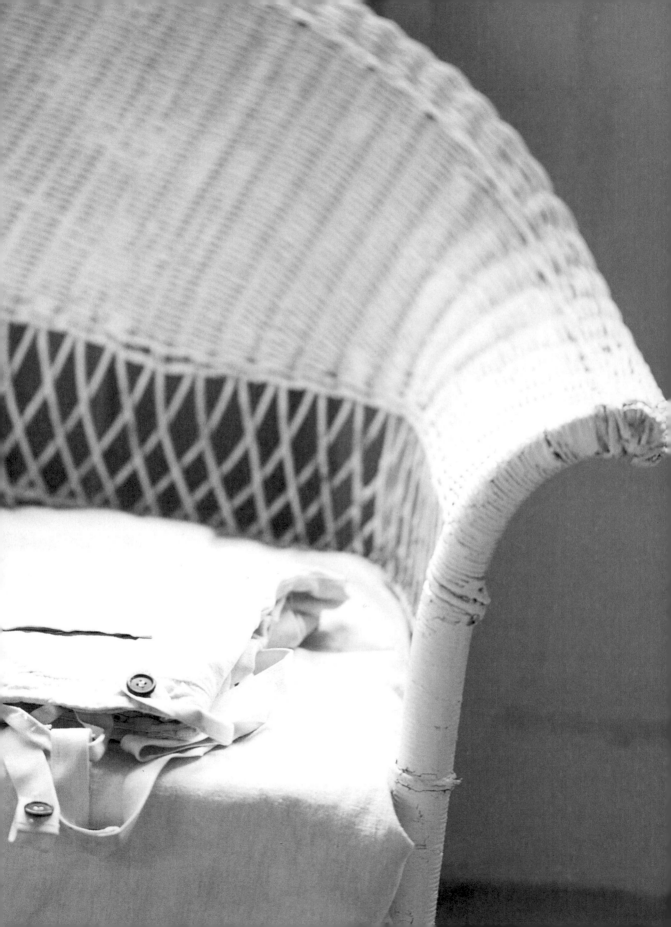

a classic find **opposite**

A Lloyd Loom style sofa fits in anywhere. A coat of white paint and a milk-coloured canvas seatcover give an instant update.

sources **left and below**

A typical brocante shop in France and a rural antiques fair. Both are wonderful sources of junk – but don't expect door-to-door delivery.

7

introduction

This book is proof that one person's junk is another's treasure. It's all about doing new, unexpected and stylish things with objects that might otherwise be thrown away or forgotten. It means choosing possessions that have already had a life and been loved rather than ones that are new, pristine and soulless. It involves accepting cracks, chips and blemishes as part of an item's attraction and as evidence that it is unique. It requires you to forget how much or how little something costs.

Although the term 'junk' is generally used to describe anything that has been discarded, some so-called rubbish is too good to be consigned to skips. Many pieces cry out to be recycled and reintegrated into our homes. Discerning devotees of junk style pick these pieces from among the clutter, upgrade them and incorporate their timeless qualities into their lives.

hunting out treasures **above**

*Be warned. There is a fine balance between
being the first to pick a bargain and being
the fool who goes home with a dud.*

recognizing potential **opposite**

*Imagine a place for each item before you buy.
Think beyond traditional uses; for example,
a galvanized bucket could hold firewood.*

The photographs in this book show real homes filled with all manner of recycled pieces that appear chic and elegant. Their owners have embraced the idea so wholeheartedly that they spend weekends searching for more examples of faded beauty. For them, using junk has become a way of life. Indeed, much of this look's appeal is that you can't just go and buy it off the shelf. The hunt itself is half the fun.

Flea markets, antiques fairs, garage sales, home and office clearances, auctions, charity outlets, salvage yards and second-hand shops: all carry the promise of intriguing finds. Each source is unpredictable and offers up its own secrets. What you end up with depends on where you look, when you get there and what your tastes are. You don't need the skills of an antiques dealer to pick up bargains.

The key is to seek out something that particularly appeals to you – a texture, a subtly aged colour, skilful craftsmanship, a decorative flourish or an object's practicality – and to make a purchase based on aesthetic values, not price tag or provenance. Salvaged items sourced with care, restored with love and introduced to your home with flair will always be its most interesting and expressive pieces. Don't be afraid to put a contemporary spin on whatever you find, mixing old with new in a way that reflects your own personal style. Happy hunting!

inspirational finds

colour

The best foil for junk style is almost always white. Its sheer simplicity and its clean, timeless look provides the perfect contemporary background for any type of junk furniture, from polished dark wood tables to classic 1950s sofas in jazzily patterned slipcovers. However, a judicious injection of strong colour as an accent on paintwork can add vibrancy to an otherwise cool scheme.

bright colours left

Yellow paint and cream walls set off the strong shapes of carefully chosen furniture.

highlights right

One strong colour on the ceiling gives this room an edge.

Choosing the right shade is vital to the success of a junk-style scheme. Harsh tones can overpower the subtlety of natural materials, and dominate organic pigments that have been dulled by the bleaching effect of the sun and a lifetime of wear and tear. Muted colours that mimic the natural effect of ageing, such as pale pastels or earthy terracottas, can offer the best complement.

muted shades

right

The mood of a room can be dictated by the colour scheme. The calm, restful atmosphere of this old Long Island barn is enhanced by the subtle shades chosen for the paint colours on the walls and the simple furniture.

metallics

left

This Paris flat has been brought up to date with white paint and an eclectic mix of metal furniture. The lime-effect finish on the old wooden beams and the floorboards echoes the chalky patina of weathered metal.

hot colours **opposite**

*Classic Robin Day chairs
in burnt orange reflectthe
bright jazzy colours typical of
1950s style..*

cupboards **right/below**

*Bold use of strong colour
can make a feature of
individual items of furniture.*

16

Surfaces touched by the gentle
ageing process are something special that
you inherit rather than buy, and that's
why the imperfections characteristic
of junk furniture and other salvaged
possessions are so precious.

Peeling wallpaper, rough plaster walls,
exposed bricks, flaking paint on a door,
a rusty bed-head, some worn-out rugs, a
bare wooden table-top and flagstones
polished by centuries of footsteps should
all be cherished because they have been
made that way by many years of use.

In deference to this, crumbling walls
can be left undecorated, the cracked or
dusty bare plaster setting the tone for
the surroundings in which you keep your
junk-shop finds. Simple flooring is best.
Bare boards, sanded down and either
polished with beeswax or limed for a
paler, more contemporary look, are an
economical option for most rooms.

surfaces

peeling paper right

*A hallway with remnants of
1950s wallpaper frames a casual
still-life of garden paraphernalia.*

the rough with the smooth left

*Cracked tiles make a practical floor; a rough
wall with a road sign brings the outside in; old
floorboards are brought up to date; years of
peeled paint create an inimitable effect.*

original walls **right**

*In this guest bedroom, the owners
have left the walls unrenovated,
so that the overall look is
a collage of different textures.*

Look out also for reclaimed tiles
and flagstones at architectural
salvage yards. Ceramic tiles
bought in small batches might
not be enough to cover a whole
floor, but they can be integrated
into larger-scale designs, or used
to create a fire-surround or to
make a splashback above a sink.
Cracked or incomplete tiles are
useful, too – they can be broken
up and laid down to create a
tessellated effect.

When it comes to old walls,
layers of paper and paint can be
partially scraped back to reveal
the decorative choices made
by generations of previous
occupants. Alternatively, you
may discover some unopened
rolls of old wallpaper in a house
clearance sale and decide to
use these to evoke the style
of a different era.

20

pattern on pattern

left

*Sections of flaking
19th-century wallpaper still
cling to the walls alongside
layers of paint and plaster,
revealing the choice of
colours and designs of all
the previous owners of the
house. The painted fireplace
is similarly unrenovated.*

21

furniture
and furnishings

Whether you are looking for something handsome or quirky, decorative or functional, industrial or domestic, ornate or unadorned, antique or contemporary – or a mix of all of them – the joy of junk furniture is that there's something for everyone. A house filled with junk furniture will have a wonderfully timeless feel, so scour sales and markets for pieces that reflect your home's unique style. As you become accustomed to shopping in this sort of environment, where a beautiful cabinet might be hiding underneath a pile of old tea chests, you'll become adept at selecting interesting items from among the mundane.

geometric lines above

The angular lines of a classic Robin Day armchair create a sharp, boxy shape.

sixties style right

This swivel chair was found in an Amsterdam office warehouse.

outside in

A weathered garden

bench was chosen for its

simple curved lines and

crusted-paint surface.

chairs

Junk shops and flea markets are filled with a wealth of chairs that have all stood the test of time. Whether you are searching for an assortment of seating for the dining room, a dressing-table stool, some metal garden furniture or a cosy armchair, you are almost certain to strike lucky. Try each piece for size before you buy, and look for indications that the chair has been comfortable enough to have been well used in the past – the sagging seat of an armchair or a wooden armrest that shines from years of use are both good signs, so don't be put off by them.

Quick and easy alterations such as adding a new cover, some plump cushions or a simple fabric throw will easily hide any major imperfections if the basic character of the piece is right.

all shapes and sizes left to right

Junk chairs come in every imaginable style: an old American rocker sits on a beachhouse deck; fancy metal seats wait to be sold in a junk lovers' paradise; a worn chair awaits a home outside a New York junk shop; a slatted French folding chair makes a great spare seat for impromptu guests; raffia chairs face the sea; a sandblasted metal chair has urban style, unusual shapes form a splintery seat; a folding chair makes a useful garden table.

slatted style left/right

*A casual arrangement of
furniture gleaned from the
garden looks surprisingly
elegant in an Amsterdam loft.*

If you are searching for dining or kitchen chairs, it is unlikely that
you will come across a complete matching set in a junk shop. Instead,

consider buying an assortment of single chairs as and when you see
them, and gradually build up an idiosyncratic selection of your own.
Look for examples that have arms and gently sloping high backs for
ultimate comfort as you dine, and make tie-on seat cushions from scraps
of fabric from the flea market to soften their look as well as their feel.
You'll find that your guests are so comfortable they will want to linger
around the table long after the meal is over.

Wicker tub chairs and metal garden chairs – especially folding
slatted ones that can be stored flat and then pressed into service if you
have unexpected guests – are all worth considering, along with more
conventional ladder-backs and carvers. Old wooden chairs that began life
in church halls and school rooms often appear in junk shops alongside
tall laboratory stools and rush-seated café chairs; all are perfect for

park chairs left

*Metal-framed wooden chairs,
such as these displayed at
an antiques fair, can make a
stylish set of dining chairs.*

28

solidity right

Chairs such as this chunky, box-seated version are so sturdily constructed that you know they still have years of useful life in them.

elegance left

Beautiful enough to be used purely for decoration, this pale wooden chair is placed in the best light to show off its glowing colour and attractive curves.

versatility left

You don't have to use chairs only as seats – placed at convenient points, they can make useful extra surfaces.

character right

A detail such as a studded leather seat can make you fall in love with a chair.

kitchen seating as they are particularly sturdy and often stackable – an asset if you are short of space.

Elegant one-off purchases such as rockers and woven Lloyd Loom chairs will look at home in a bedroom or bathroom, creating a quiet corner in which to relax.

Office clearances are a good source of seating for workrooms. Adjustable architects' chairs and leather-covered swivel chairs are extremely practical as well as being better looking and more unusual than modern options. Make sure that you buy one that is the correct height for use with your desk so you will be able to work in comfort as well as in style.

the main feature

A kitsch 1950s chair becomes
a focal point in the corner
of this otherwise minimally
decorated apartment.

benches and sofas

Buying a new sofa can be an expensive business. so a junk-shop alternative, even if it needs a few repairs, is likely to be a good bargain. Metal-framed day beds, benches and chaises longues are also much sought-after because they are sociable pieces of furniture that give a room an air of casual relaxation, especially when piled high with an inviting assortment of cushions or strewn with old rugs or kilims.

A generous seating arrangement is indispensable in a sitting room, but it is also wonderful in the sort of kitchen that is the hub of family life, in a quiet bedroom where you might retreat with a book, in a corner of a roomy bathroom, or in a study.

Whichever part of the house a sofa is destined for, comfort should be your priority when you are on the lookout for the best buys. Sprawl out on sofas before you part with any money to make sure that they are as comfortable as they are good-looking. To ensure that wooden, wicker and metal-framed benches meet the same criteria, buy and fit some feather-filled squabs. The bench can then be used as overflow seating in the sitting room or space-saving seating alongside a rectangular dining table — perfect for children to use for family meals.

sackcloth **opposite**

The cushions and bolster for this pretty bench have been designed to set off the stitched strip and logo of these old French flour sacks.

reinventing the wheel **above**

An old cartwheel rescued from a sale of farming implements becomes a work of art when it is placed in an interior setting.

cover story **right**

Cream linen sheets help to protect a generous sofa from the rigours of family life in this Dutch living room.

Leather-covered sofas age beautifully and, along with classic Chesterfields and Knoles, are the ultimate in shabby chic. You may be lucky enough to find one at a flea market that needs only the odd patch here and there to make it serviceable.

To hide leaking stuffing or a tatty fitted cover, make some slipcovers from a fabric that complements the sofa's faded look, or shroud the whole thing in a swathe of cloth – ignore the folds and creases and simply tuck in the edges. Look for faded curtains, old sack cloth, shawls and bedspreads with a lived-in look, and your 'new' upholstery will not detract from the sofa's dated charm.

creased up **above**

Provided that the framework
is sound, any old sofa can be
given a new lease of life with
a simple cream canvas cover.

bright white

White unifies this eclectic mix of junk furniture for a modern look. The decorative fluted table legs contrast with the cool swivel chairs.

tables

Create your own tables from flea-market finds such as vintage travel trunks, old cable reels, scrubbed plank benches and simple trestles. With such diversity of choice, junk shops should be able to provide every surface you will ever need, from dining tables and bedside cabinets to makeshift desks.

For kitchens, it's hard to beat old pine refectory tables for sheer practicality — and they are easy to find in all shapes and sizes. A coat of tough varnish will protect your table against damage, whether the source of danger is children's crayons or hot pans. Choose the biggest table your kitchen can accommodate, bearing in mind that this surface is likely to get used for hobbies, laptop activities and reading the newspaper as well as at mealtimes and for preparing food.

For smaller spaces, drop-leaf tables are more versatile. They can accommodate large gatherings when necessary, while those with drawers are useful for extra storage.

Small steel-topped tables and butcher's blocks are also good for providing an extra work surface when space is at a premium.

sweet dreams
An old garden table with twisted metal legs appears quite at home beside a bed.

If your kitchen space is limited, look out for a pretty marble-topped café table with cast-iron legs or a wicker side table that will fit snugly into a corner and enable two people to eat there comfortably. It's also useful to have a small table in the hallway where you can keep keys and post, place a lamp, or display a generous vase of fresh flowers for an immediate welcome. Try to find an unusual piece of furniture that will make a striking first impression: a sewing-machine bench, an ornate metal-framed table with a glass top or a decorative wooden console will establish the junk-style look as soon as you step inside the front door.

Occasional tables are indispensable in the sitting room for taking tea by the fire or keeping your book beside a favourite armchair, so explore junk shops and yard sales for anything from small wooden stools and folding butler's-tray tables to wooden tea trolleys and stacking coffee tables.

Many of these table options also work well in bedrooms as alternatives to conventional matching bedside cabinets or in the bathroom piled with fresh linens or baskets of soaps.

If you unearth something at a flea market that really is past its best but still has some quality about it that appeals to you, there's a good chance that it will still come in handy in the garden or potting shed as a workbench or plant stand.

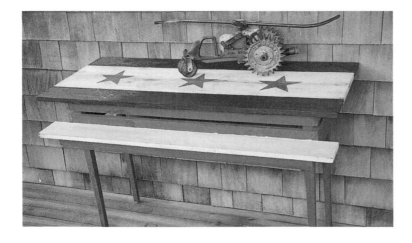

recycling left/right

A huge cable wheel has been given a new life as a work table in a designer's Paris apartment, while a sewing-machine stand, complete with foot pedal, has been transformed into an unusual side table.

stars and stripes
far left

National pride obviously dictated the decoration for this brightly painted two-tier table.

lucky find left

A simple cross-leg trestle is the most basic table you will find. Its versatile shape means that it will work well in any situation.

piano cover left

A pretty striped cotton in French blue contrasts with blue checks on the chair and helps to disguise a piano.

fabrics

Junk shops are filled with textiles such as curtains, blankets, mattress tickings, quilts, bed linens, lace and even fabric remnants of all sizes in innumerable colours, weights, textures and patterns. The inimitable look and feel of faded chintz, old velvet, time-softened linens and kitsch prints will make your rooms feel snug and lived in, so blend together a variety of these fabrics, mixing them with modern pieces if you like.

Use more precious pieces sparingly in a position where they can take pride of place and allow less costly ones to hang in generous folds. Vintage fabrics can be left unironed, threadbare or patched to give your surroundings an air of relaxed living.

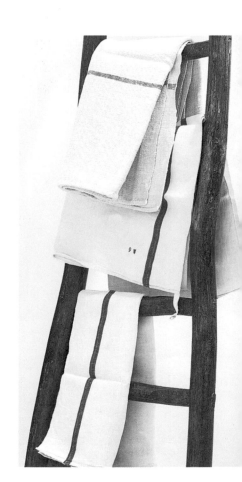

ticking over left

Traditional mattress ticking comes in a huge range of colours and looks great when integrated with complementary patterns, as here.

ladder of success right

An old ladder simply propped up against a wall makes an original towel rail, useful in the bathroom or the kitchen.

Vintage fabrics have a charm that cannot be replicated by modern materials, however faithful fabric companies may be in replicating old designs. The fabrics that survive years of good service relatively intact tend to be the durable ones. They are usually made from natural rather than man-made fibres, and they are an appropriate complement to the other natural textures, such as wood, that are a key part of junk style.

The authentic feel of antique linen or lace or soft woollen blankets that have been washed so many times the nap has worn smooth more than compensates for a frayed edge or occasional small hole. Paisleys,

rambling roses below

A boldly patterned curtain spread over a dormitory bed transforms the mood of the room.

a touch of lace above

Recycled curtains also provide a delicate lacy undersheet beneath the top cover.

florals, stripes and checks bring splashes of pattern to otherwise subtly decorated rooms, often inspiring their overall colour schemes. Even the most overblown chintz will look charming rather than overpowering when surrounded by the casual restraint of junk style.

So drape dining tables with layers of linen and lace for a touch of faded grandeur; dress beds with antique linens, soft counterpanes and feather-filled bolsters; cover sofas and chairs with fabrics such as sensual silk, knobbly chenille, starched cotton and warm wool to enhance their comfortable appeal.

floral charm **below**

This pretty bedcover, which began life as a curtain, was found in a junk-shop rummage basket.

violets **above**

Subtle florals, such as this 1950s design, can soften an otherwise coolly decorated room.

pure white **this page**

All-white bed linen lends a monastic feel to a room. For extra warmth, add woollen blankets, as Peter Hone has on this 19th-century travelling bed (below), bought for his restored-grainstore home.

picnic checks **opposite**

Faded woollen blankets in contrasting pale pastels were used to re-upholster this pair of classic armchairs with rounded arms. The chairs are soft, comfortable oases in a minimalist London loft.

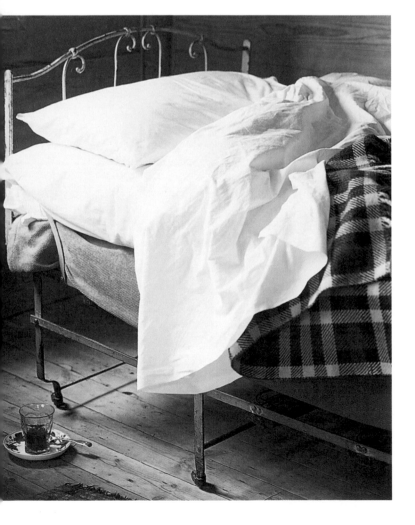

To complement rich vintage textiles, buy new lengths of utility fabrics such as gingham, striped ticking, sheeting, muslin or canvas. These are cheap enough to use in large quantities – make them up into slipcovers or sew them into a border to make a small treasured piece of fabric a more workable size. Since they are timeless, they blend well with older, more decorative fabrics. Try mixing new gingham with a faded floral, a pristine ticking with some old checks, an elegant damask with some unbleached cotton, or a length of linen with a panel of antique lace.

Diehard recyclers do what generations have done before them when they have finished sewing; they collect any leftover scraps to make into a patchwork quilt.

pots of style **opposite**

Kitchen scales and salt pots sit among storage jars and bottles in a monochrome collection of kitchenware.

boxed in **left**

Plenty of dents and a rusty, peeling-paint finish simply enhance the charm of these old storage tins.

containers
and storage

45

For innovative storage solutions, junk shops make wonderful hunting grounds. From boxes and baskets to cabinets and shelving, these pieces are essential additions to any well-organized home, whether you like to maintain a minimalist, clean and contemporary look or to fill your home with a wonderful array of treasured clutter. Search for both conventional and unusual pieces to house your possessions. Useful finds include enamel tins and bread bins, wooden crates, medicine chests, baker's racks, butcher's hooks and an assortment of basketware.

great crates **right**

Baskets and wine crates complete with original lettering are an economical storage solution.

small storage

Before the days of mass production and man-made materials, people took great care to market everything from vegetables to soap powder in tins, trays, bags, crates, racks, barrels, boxes and baskets that were carefully packaged and often labelled with beautiful lettering to advertise their contents and the producer's identity. They were made to be so durable that many still survive today, frequently cropping up among the junk at stalls and markets after years of being shut away in attics and cellars. All deserve to be given a new lease of life, so buy them to use for storage all around the home as well as in the garden. They are far more desirable than the crude replica tins and baskets that are now on the market in response to a revived interest in period pieces.

Wooden grocer's trays and vegetable crates are useful for storing toys in a playroom, displaying plants in a conservatory, growing herbs on the kitchen windowsill and holding supplies of dried goods in the kitchen. Brightly painted logos, especially ones that reveal an exotic past, are most sought after. Old shopping bags, bicycle panniers, picnic hampers and fisherman's baskets

enamelware right
Enamel kitchenware, very popular in the 1930s, is still going strong today.

egg box left
A metal box originally used to store eggs has found a new home as a place to keep paperwork and letters.

46

well dressed **above**

A utilitarian metal rail is a perfect makeshift wardrobe, allowing a wonderful array of second-hand clothes to be on permanent show.

baskets **far right**

Baskets come in handy for storing bulbs in the shed or vegetables in the kitchen — or even to house sleeping kittens

bird houses **right**

A row of narrow wooden bird houses adds a quirky touch to a basic set of painted wooden drawers. If some drawers in a unit are missing, utilize the empty spaces to display favourite objects.

barrels **right**

A stack of wooden barrels wait to be recycled as anything from umbrella stands to laundry baskets.

are covetable for their intricate workmanship as well as for their versatility. Fill them with shoes for under-bed storage or with logs for placing beside the fire, or line them with fabric and use them for laundry. A fraying handle or a unravelled edge can either be carefully repaired or left as it is to add to the charm.

Enamel tins often appear among kitchenalia in junk stores — sometimes labelled 'flour' or 'sugar', sometimes striped or with coloured lids. French markets offer similar items in which to keep *'farine'* and *'sucre'* — these are particularly sought after for recreating rural Provençal style or faded Parisian chic. A mismatched assortment can look wonderful on a kitchen shelf and are just as useful today as they were originally.

Metal trunks, old suitcases and leather collar and hat boxes can be filled with clothes, book and papers, then piled up on top of a wardrobe or under a dressing table to create an eye-catching display as well as making the most of a limited space and reviving age-old household practice. For bathrooms, seek out wooden drying racks, linen presses and laundry baskets to store towels, and small shelving units and glass bottles for toiletries.

Plan chests, bookcases of all shapes and sizes and wooden crates are ideal for books and magazines. You can also use them to conceal the accumulations of modern life, such as CDs and DVDs, that detract froml the clean lines of the junk-style look, while a metal filing cabinet will swallow up household papers, bills and documents.

a good read below far left

A collection of books and glassware is enticingly displayed on open shelves.

kept on file below left

Metal filing-card boxes are indispensable for the home office or workroom.

garden display below

A rickety wooden baker's stand makes an attractive feature in a sheltered outdoor corner. It is a convenient place to store tools and equipment and to display fruit and vegetables freshly picked from the garden.

49

safe as houses **right**

An old-fashioned meat safe offers a stylish way to expand kitchen storage.

herb garden **left**

For a miniature kitchen garden, drill holes in the base of a wooden crate and plant it with a variety of culinary herbs.

portable **below**

A shallow-sided crate can be used as an impromptu tray.

Glass-fronted cabinets and open shelves can be useful all around the house. Look out for shop fittings such as drapers' display counters with glass-fronted drawers for original storage units, while in the bedroom a single free-standing metal clothes rail can look stylish. Other options for original and functional storage include blanket boxes, old leather suitcases and even dressmaker's dummies. In awkward spaces such as halls, try pegs, hat stands, drawstring shoe-bags and metal shelving.

Old panelled wooden doors, in plentiful supply at flea markets, can be fixed over existing alcoves and recesses – for example, under the stairs – to make extra cupboards that look as if they have been there for years. Equipped with shelves or rows of hooks, they make ideal places to store linen, coats and household equipment.

cupboard love **left**

*An ornate, painted wall
cupboard is lined with
illustrations taken from
an old recipe book.*

very cool **opposite, above**

*Stripped of its enamelled
surface, a classic refrigerator
shows off its sleek lines in
bright stainless steel.*

52

cupboards

With a little imagination, the great variety of containers for sale in
flea markets and at auctions can be seen as the starting point for
ingenious, attractive storage. For example, an old pie safe would
make a convenient place to store crockery, a pine wardrobe could
become a pantry, and a wooden cabinet could find a new role in
the bathroom stacked high with towels.

Generously proportioned cupboards are at a premium in junk
shops because they are such a practical and handsome addition
to the home, especially in the bedroom, where a free-standing,
French-style *armoire* or a rough-and-ready pine wardrobe can be
stylish. Corner cabinets should also be snapped up as they will
allow you to make the most of awkward spaces that would
otherwise be wasted. Details such as carving, decorative moulding,
coloured glass insets, a mirrored front panel and attractive door
furniture all make a purchase worthwhile.

loaded up **below**

*Whatever style of cupboard
you are looking for, flea
markets are bound provide
an abundance of choice.*

Easier to carry back from your junk shop forays are smaller cupboards, which are useful throughout the house for storing anything from clothes and stationery to food. Glass-fronted cabinets are ideal if you are happy to put the contents of the cupboard on show. Arrange what's inside attractively – whether it is tins of baked beans or your best crockery – to make the most of the display.

Revamping your cupboards with new or reclaimed door knobs, pull handles and decorative and unusual brass or iron hinges, or even just polishing up the existing ones with steel wool, can work wonders, as can replacing cracked or warped door panels with etched or clear glass, chicken wire or a length of fabric gathered on a wire.

53

picture of style **below**

Pale, neutral colours define the decorative style In the Paris apartment of designer Roxanne Beis. This subtly bleached, metal-trimmed cupboard fits in perfectly.

in the garden **below**

No junk item should be regarded as too precious for outdoor life – this handsome flower-topped armoire, for example, makes an intriguing garden feature.

classic **below**

A simple painted closet furnishes a house on Long Island. Flea-market finds such as wooden fruit boxes and an old sign add character and a touch of humour.

lamps
and lighting

Lighting has a huge impact on the way we feel about a room and the way we see the objects that fill it. Even the no-frills approach of a simply shaded bulb or a naked candle flame has a profound effect on its atmosphere. So when you are creating a specific look from your junk-shop finds, don't ignore details such as lighting. While there is no need to restrict yourself to one style or period, you should strive to be sympathetic to the overall look, and bear in mind that many modern light fittings will be inappropriate. Installing decorative light fixtures and fittings obtained from your favourite stalls and markets will enhance the junk-style character of your home.

rise and fall

This elegant, adjustable pendant light proves that, if you want versatility, you don't have to limit your choice to a modern fitting.

lights fantastic

Search flea markets for period light fittings such as wirework candleholders, a French glass shade to hang over a dining table or a clip-on metal spot lamp that is perfect for task lighting in the kitchen.

Salvage yards and second-hand outlets are usually well stocked with original light fixtures and fittings, many of which will have been ripped out of old buildings in the name of modernization. But the majority of these items are still fully functional and they can last another lifetime if they are rescued and reused.

Second-hand electric light fixtures should always be checked and installed by a qualified electrician, so that any worn or damaged wiring or connections can be replaced. Once their safety has been certified, old fixtures can do their job more stylishly then their

modern equivalents, many of which are too hi-tech in design to combine easily with the other, more traditional junk elements in your home.

The warmth and romance of candlelight harmonizes perfectly with the relaxed character of junk style, so try to use it wherever possible. Candle-holders are available in numerous different forms, from containers designed

specifically for the job to old jam jars adapted for the purpose. For a decorative flourish, vintage pewter candlesticks, perhaps dented or worn smooth by years of polishing, can often be found relatively cheaply among grander, more expensive antiques. More rustic options include sturdy metal hurricane lamps and storm lanterns, which look great on

a good sign **right**

As well as buying old lights, you can adapt other junk items to camouflage modern light fittings. French lighting designer Alexis Aufray made this highly original light fitting out of an old rusted-metal road sign. The bulb behind floods the wall with light.

the mantelpiece or table, but which are also useful outside on summer evenings.

Before you set off on your first foraging expedition, plan the lighting scheme for each room in the house, deciding what type and style of fittings you need and where they will go. Each room should have something to give general or ambient lighting – a central pendant, for example. There should also be individual task lights

candle light **below**

A quintet of bulbous storm lanterns made from thick glass have been suspended from a beam on simple wire hangers.

on the road **bottom**

A portable lamp once used by a roadworker now illuminates a table at Woolloomooloo restaurant in Avignon, France.

storm front **bottom**

Used to light an alfresco meal or simply as outdoor decoration, hurricane lamps such as these are romantic and stylish.

gaslight **below**

A small round mirror reflects the rusted-metal wick control of an old gas-light fitting with its original glass lantern.

57

over desks, beside armchairs and in kitchens to make studying, reading or cooking easier. Finally, you will need some sort of accent lighting to draw the eye towards particular areas that you wish to highlight, such as a work of art or an attractive collection of objects on display.

Lighting to fulfil all of these roles – plus any pieces you fall in love with on the spot for their purely decorative qualities and determine to find a place for as soon as you return home – can easily be found by sifting through junk shops.

Finding a coloured or plain glass-drop chandelier might well be one of the highlights of your search – with a bit of cleaning, and perhaps a replacement glass-drop here and there, it will give off a delicate twinkling light that is grand but never gaudy. Hang it in conventional

take the floor **below**

A chair beside an open fire, with an ornate floor lamp to give illumination, is the ideal place to relax with a good book. A model dog provides suitably silent company.

58

style over a dining table or somewhere more unusual, such as a bathroom, to give an air of opulence. If you decide to use a chandelier purely as a beautifully decorative object rather than having it wired to the electricity supply for use as a light, hang it near a source of natural illumination such as window so the glass drops catch and reflect the sunlight. Candelabras can make a similarly grand statement, but remember that lighted candles should never be left unattended, and the smoke can leave stains on a plain white ceiling.

Look out, too, for glass or ceramic up-lighters that will wash an entire wall with gentle light, and for elegant standard lamps, with or without their original shades. Pleated shades to fit — silk if you are lucky, paper if you are not — can often be found separately, along with an assortment of other shades in glass, metal, parchment, wicker or fabric. These can either be paired off with other lamp bases you might find or easily adapted to use with pendant fittings. Wall sconces — some incorporating candle-holders, others fitted with kitsch flame-shaped bulbs — are also much sought after, especially wrought-iron models in ornate floral or foliage designs.

The best finds are always the classics designs, and in this case of lighting these are old adjustable anglepoise desk lamps, tall metal standard lamps with extending arms and traditional brass picture lights.

clear your desk **top**

Garage sales are a good source of adjustable desk lamps. Check that the springs are sound — too tight and the arms won't budge; too loose and your lamp will flop.

a good angle **above**

Anglepoise lamps are essential desk accessories in both traditional and contemporary offices. Their flexible and stylish design has changed little over the years.

mix and match left

Keep your eyes open for pieces of cheap glassware and cutlery for everyday use.

glass, china
and ceramics

decoration opposite

A selection of intricately patterned spoons makes a pretty still life on an ornate glass dish. Though the cutlery is mismatched, the styles are similar enough to make a harmonious whole.

something special right

Glass vases, dishes and cake plates are useful one-off purchases. They might seem kitsch in isolation, but together they make a charming group.

The delicate floral china plates and cut-glass vases that were cherished by our grandmothers are now fashionable once again and are an integral part of junk style. Think of a pitcher filled with flowers, a china bowl planted with hyacinths, a shelf laden with dishes, a dresser piled high with earthenware or a table set with an assortment of china, and you'll capture the right look. Prices for this kind of item are very reasonable, so it is not hard to build up an impressively diverse collection for everyday use or for decoration. Sorting through piles of plates, searching for an unusual design, and imagining how a glass bottle would look after it has been cleaned, adds to the enjoyment.

62

Gone are the days when we had to have a fully matching dinner service. Now, table settings with character can comprise mismatched plates, odd glasses and a variety of pieces of cutlery, even when entertaining. Whether you are hosting a dinner party or just having a few friends around for coffee, a casual assortment of glass and china will make it an easy-going affair.

Tableware makes up only a fraction of the pieces you are likely to come across. If you spot a bowl-and-pitcher set, a dish or some dressing-table china, your junk-shop finds could also adorn your bathroom and bedroom. Similarly, bottles and jars

all set **right**

Among more ordinary china pieces, you may be lucky enough to find a complete dinner set.

shelf life **left**

Simple wooden shelving is used to display china plates amassed over many years.

something fishy
opposite, top left

This collection of china has a seaside theme, making it witty as well as pretty.

bargains
opposite, below left

Boxes of inexpensive crockery await the bargain hunter at New York shop Fishs Eddy.

user-friendly **right**

Flea-market finds are not just for show – use them for everyday meals and you'll appreciate them to the full.

that were discarded years ago, when the milk, medicine or ginger beer ran out, often find their way back into the home via garage or yard sales and house clearances. Use them to display a single stem or lined up en masse on a windowsill. Coloured glass looks particularly good when it filters shafts of sunlight beside a window, so search for old bottles in vivid shades of cobalt blue, soft aqua, deep green or glowing amber. Embossed lettering and original labels, plus lids, stoppers and corks, add to their charm.

63

simple flowers **below**

Plain glassware often makes
possible the prettiest floral
arrangements. Display single
stems in clear tumblers.

big is beautiful **below**

Oversized containers are
perfect for large flowers. This
narrow-necked demi-john
easily supports a huge allium.

64

cocktail kitsch **right**

Plastic 1950s glamour-girl
swizzle sticks are a perfect
match for these modern
classic tumblers.

rosy outlook **far right**

For impromptu displays all
around the house, fill
cut-glass glasses with
seasonal flowers.

season to taste left

A row of inexpensive salt shakers make an unpretentious and eye-catching display on a shelf in a seaside home.

high life below

Old glass bottles with their original spring-loaded stoppers are arranged in a prominent position on top of a cupboard.

blue mood above left

An antique cachepot is now home to a simple display of hedgerow flowers.

in bloom left/far left

Antiques and flowers are combined at the Long Island florists Potted Gardens.

lock and key right

Junk collections are all about style rather than cost. This array of old lock barrels has aesthetic rather than monetary value.

on show left

The possessions that fill a house reflect the owner's character and interests. The contents of artist Yuri Kuper's converted barn in Normandy, France, reveal his fondness for architectural prints and found objects, ranging in this case from a pestle and mortar to a pair of discarded boots.

collections
and collectables

Anything can provide the starting point for a collection of junk objects, from an array of old tobacco tins to a handful of lead fishing weights. Once you have identified something you covet, every subsequent trip to a junk shop will have more momentum because it might reveal just the thing you have been looking for. A collection speaks volumes about the person who has amassed it, and quirky and highly idiosyncratic items often become the most obsessively sought after. The hunt for picture books, pearl buttons, board games, egg whisks, hats or bird cages can become all-consuming; when arranged in displays around the house, these objects add lovely witty touches.

beside the sea **right**

This collection of fishing weights

turned up in a local charity shop.

tin ware **right**

This group of battered tins is on show in Yuri Kuper's loft home in New York City.

garden shed **below**

The best collector's items may be lying forgotten in a shed. Search out bell jars, flower pots and watering-can roses.

68

More mundane and familiar objects are also worth collecting, and they are very easy to pick up at car-boot or yard sales. The perennial favourite is kitchenware, and some covetable household utensils, such as kettles and weighing scales, can earn their keep as well as enlarge your collection if they are still in working order.

Garden tools are another popular option, especially old cloches, terracotta pots and trugs, which can either adorn a conservatory or be pressed back into service.

Not everyone who spends hours searching for the perfect piece to add to their collection ends up with a house full of clutter. Collecting can be compatible with a desire for a minimalist interior. Whatever look you want to create, be precise: discretion and theming are the keys to making discerning purchases from the myriad examples of junk on offer.

handiwork left

Tools become decorative items in their own right when hung up on a wall; the more evidence of their past use the better.

flat out above

Discerning collectors focus on one class of objects – such as antique flat-irons – and look for additions wherever they go.

in stitches **right**

A still-life is created from a collection of old sewing paraphernalia – much still in its original delightful packaging.

a cut above **below**

Show off your treasures behind glass. Dressmakers' tools and bright napkins go on display in two handsome jars.

well spun **above**

The natural hues of these old silk threads, some still threaded on factory-sized spools, form another haberdashery-inspired collection.

hat stand

An old fruit-picking
ladder is used to
display a collection
of hats in painter
Charlotte Culot's
Provençal home.

outside interest **far left**

Multi-coloured plaster-relief plaques depicting various mythological scenes decorate the walls of an outbuilding.

ultra marine **left**

Flying birds, a wooden sailing boat and some spades create a distinctly nautical display in a seaside home.

73

still life **below**

Dried seed heads, ceramics, shells and pictures are the simple ingredients that bring a shelf to life.

decoration
and display

Finding ways to arrange the items you have collected from junk shops is great fun. The more innovative and creative your displays the better, since they invite you to look at old objects in a new light, as well as allowing you to decorate your home with an interesting personal touch.

Corner cupboards, narrow shelves, small cubby holes and old wooden printer's boxes are tailor-made for small-scale arrangements. Displays of belongings make a room feel lived in, so keep them fresh by changing them whenever the mood takes you – or when a buying trip forces you to move things to make room for another irresistible treasure.

Look out for glazed box frames and glass-fronted cabinets to show off tiny trinkets. Bigger items, especially in the kitchen and the pantry, can be hung from ceiling racks and wooden airers. Some successful displays arrange like with like so you can enjoy their similarities: imagine the effect of seeing a row of identical clear-glass apothecary jars on a bathroom cabinet, or a shelf of spongeware pitchers. Others work well because of the deliberate juxtaposition of different styles, colours and textures. You might love the contrast between contemporary ceramics and old porcelain, or between kitsch artificial flowers and brass candlesticks.

three of a kind **above**

*Wooden spades are propped
up against the wood-panelled
wall of a beach house.*

holy order **left**

*Religious icons fill a shrine-
like wooden cupboard in a
home in Amsterdam.*

gallery **right/overleaf**

*A rusty saw embellished with
wonderful lettering has been
given pride of place on a
white wall, while treasures
varying from a life buoy to a
battered shoe last can be
used as adornment
(next page).*

beach finds **above**

*Use the treasures from
your beachcombing
expeditions to cover a
selection of boxes.*

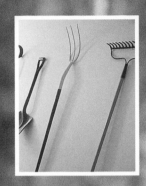

found objects

Junk addicts keep their eyes open for objects of interest wherever they go. Whether you are spending the day lazing on a beach, digging in the garden or walking in the woods, there's a good chance that you might discover a natural wonder or some man-made object, discarded long ago, that can become a treasure in its own right. It is particularly satisfying to collect these things because they are close at hand, easy to find and – best of all – absolutely free. Beachcombing is as much fun for children discovering the joys of the seaside for the first time as it is for adults recapturing childhood memories.

natural selection above

A walk in the woods can reveal any number of natural finds, from feathers to textural stones.

mantelpiece right

These skulls were found in the Camargue and in Africa, while the antlers are from Provence.

wooden wonders **above**

Interesting pieces of driftwood,
wooden bowls and undressed
stone surfaces give a natural
look in a bathroom.

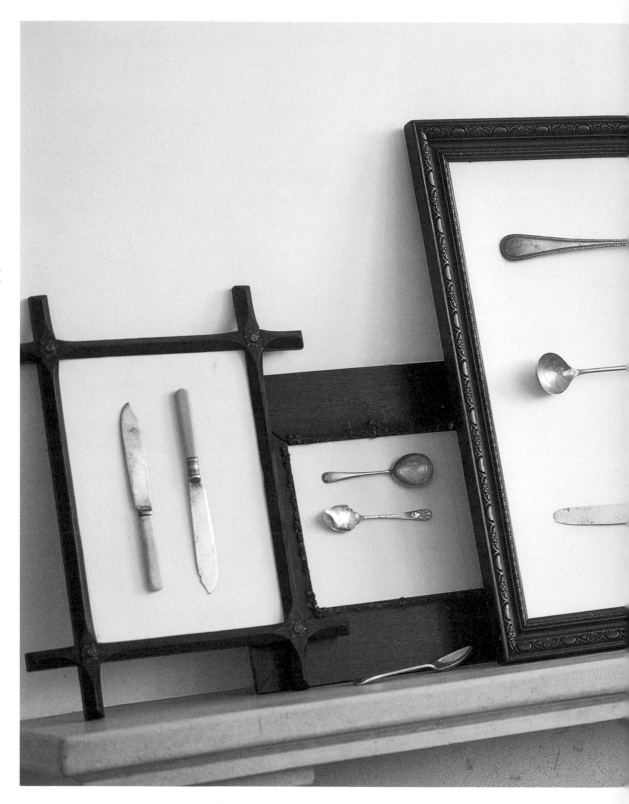

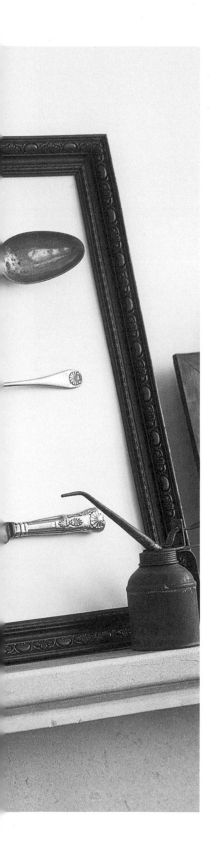

in the frame **left**

Odd pieces of cutlery find a new home mounted on white cardboard and displayed in second-hand frames.

in full bloom **above right**

An old wooden barrow, complete with its original wheel, has been permanently parked and planted to make an unusual container garden.

hidden potential **right**

Another wheelbarrow sits forgotten in an outhouse awaiting a similar transformation.

Scan the high-water mark and you might find jewel-like pieces of sea-smoothed glass washed up alongside delicate feathers, gnarled and twisted lengths of sculptural driftwood, chunks of flint and perhaps a fisherman's basket or float.

As they turn over the soil, gardeners – particularly in gardens attached to old houses – are accustomed to unearthing a wealth of interesting objects. Fragments of pottery, a section of glazed tile, a cup handle or a section of clay pipe, are all worth keeping. As well as being beautifully made and lovely to look at, these objects can also give a fascinating insight into the local history of the area in which you live. Elsewhere in the garden, old flower pots and wrought-iron brackets are waiting to be discovered and appreciated. Luckier finds include discarded garden tools, such as rusted rakes and spades, or even an old wheelbarrow. These can be turned into permanent decorative features in the garden or even brought into the house to be shown off.

82

pots of colour **above**

Mottle-glazed ceramic pots are ideal for containing all sorts of floral specimens, short or tall.

indoor garden **above**

Bring terracotta pots in from the potting shed and enjoy the flowers while they are in bloom.

flowers

A vase of fresh flowers will bring instant warmth to a room filled with junk furniture. Flawless and relatively short-lived, floral displays provide a graceful counterpoint to the imperfections and timelessness of old furniture. The vivid shades introduce a note of intense colour that will lift the spirits, and such an injection of vitality can be particularly welcome in neutral room schemes.

formal or informal **left/above**

A stemmed dish makes a perfect table centrepiece, while a galvanized jug creates a more casual display.

growing interest **inset**

*Nature has overwhelmed
a rusty garden chair.*

delicate touch

*Plain shapes and clear glass
are best for simple flowers.*

new life **left**

*An old metal kettle is now
home to a cluster of cheerful
pansies, while an enamel jug
plays host to hydrangeas.*

spike **below**

*Who says plants thrive only in
clay pots? They will be happy
in all manner of containers,
given proper drainage holes.*

pitcher perfect below

Place a few sprays of the same type of flower in different vases close together for a charming group.

well contained right

Junk finds such as these buckets make perfect vases. The more unexpected the container the better.

living with
junk

classics **left**

Corbusier-designed chairs
– 20th-century classics –
mingle happily with humbler
flea-market furniture in
a Paris apartment.

living
and dining

Once you have tracked down the best second-hand furniture, fabrics and accessories you can find, it's time to put all the elements together to create a home that looks good and is easy to live in. There are no rules – no strictures about making exact matches or even about using items for the purpose they were originally designed. One of the pleasures of using junk is that pieces salvaged from a former life bring some of that character with them – but junk style is not a wallow in nostalgia or about faithfully recreating replicas of historical interiors. It is a look that is very much of the moment.

back to basics **right**

Decoration is minimal in this 17th-century
grainstore or 'hutt', as it is known – only the
Duke of Gloucester's old picnic hamper and
a couple of casual shirts adorn the wall.

living with junk

Junk-style interiors are fresh and modern. The less clutter there is, the better able you are to appreciate the clean lines of chairs and tables chosen for their strong shapes. Often it is a particular colour, shape or texture that will have attracted you to a second-hand item in the first place – whether it's the warm glow of aged wood patinated with the scars of years of use or the jewel-like shine of coloured glass – so you will want to show off your finds to their best advantage.

Spontaneity and a lack of pretension are at the heart of junk style. Whatever pieces you find will speak for themselves, establishing their own unique style and making everyone who enters your living space feel completely and utterly at home.

90

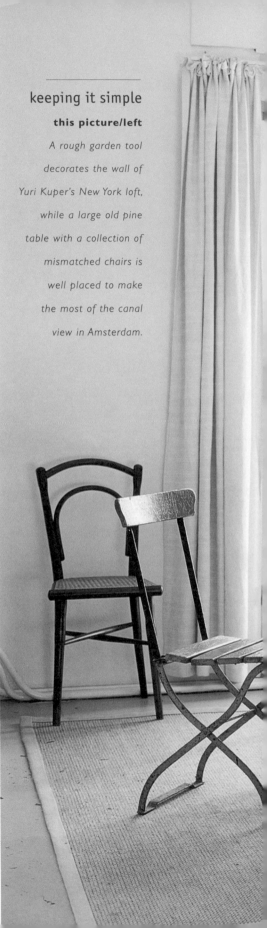

keeping it simple
this picture/left
A rough garden tool decorates the wall of Yuri Kuper's New York loft, while a large old pine table with a collection of mismatched chairs is well placed to make the most of the canal view in Amsterdam.

92

For a spacious look with restrained adornment, decorate your living and dining areas with white walls and a few carefully selected treasures. For a busier feel, use rich shades and introduce the paintings and quirky *objets d'art* that you have picked up over the years.

If there is space for two or even three sofas, so much the better. Arrange them so that they face one another, perhaps alongside a couple of slouchy armchairs, to make a sociable group. Despite the variety of shapes, sizes and different colours and design of the worn upholstery fabrics, the room will feel harmonious as each of the elements in it is laid-back and unaffected.

long table **left**

Charlotte Culot bought her generously proportioned dining table from a flea market in Ardèche, France.

rural retreat **far left**

This reclaimed 17th-century country grainstore is furnished with a charming hotchpotch of finds.

eating out **below**

Restoration was kept to a minimum when stylish restaurant Woolloomooloo in Avignon was converted from an old print works.

93

If you are lucky enough to have a fireplace make this the room's focus by arranging your sofas and chairs around it. Look out for old fire-irons, screens, metal fenders and coal scuttles to set in the hearth to complete the picture. Add extra comfort and convenience by introducing other junk purchases such as footstools and occasional tables, along with an assortment of feather-filled cushions, colourful throws and warm tartan blankets. Look out for rag mats and woven hearth rugs to give the room yet another layer of softness.

Whether you have a separate dining area or tend to eat in the sitting room or kitchen, every house should have a special place set aside for the enjoyment of food, from family lunches to dinner

on the bench left

Long benches, whether they started life as garden furniture or even as church pews, are very versatile in dining rooms because they can seat so many people.

wood right

The beauty of wooden furniture is that whatever it is made of, from pine to oak, and whatever the finish or colour, it will always look good with other wooden furniture.

with friends. Junk style creates a warm and inviting look that is a far cry from the stuffiness of a formal dining room. Here, no one has to stand on ceremony because the table is rough-and-ready pine rather than polished mahogany, the candlesticks are hand-blown glass rather than solid silver, and the tablecloth is not starched white damask but a simple length of gingham.

Table settings can be as plain or as ornate as you like – even at its most decorative, junk style is never overwhelming. At one end of the spectrum, create a no-frills approach with a bare wooden table top set with plain white china in a mixture of weights and shapes, old linen napkins, plain stainless-steel cutlery, chunky tumblers and a jug of flowers. For special occasions, old lace can form the backdrop for floral china, assorted bone-handled silver cutlery, elegant cut-glass goblets and a stemmed crystal dish piled high with fruit as a centrepiece.

kitchens

People tend to gather in the kitchen because it is a place of warmth, somewhere where they can go to enjoy good company as well as nourishment, where conversations, meals, work, food preparation and leisure activities can all happily take place alongside one another.

take a seat **opposite**

Sturdy church chairs, such as these inherited from a Sunday School, make excellent kitchen seating.

any old iron **below**

Aluminium kettles and colanders can be found in abundance.

pots and pans far left

This matching set of aluminium saucepans with white handles was found in a Paris flea market.

retro chic left

Designer Roxanne Beis loved the 1940s cupboards she inherited with her Paris flat — so much she designed her kitchen around them.

Kitchen junk looks at home even in a modern setting. It makes a lovely contrast to stainless-steel cookers and fitted units, and gives authenticity to retro kitchens inspired by, for example, 1940s or 1950s style. You might find yourself being more selective and choosing fewer pieces than you would for a more country-style kitchen, but the junk elements you do include will really stand out against the room's cool, clean lines.

It can be highly enjoyable to scour markets and salerooms in search of early kitchen gadgets. Pieces dating from decades ago, such as meat mincers, coffee grinders, juicers, nutcrackers, cream-makers and weighing scales with their sets of brass or iron weights, were often so well designed and sturdily built that they are still going strong today. As well as being better looking than many of today's plastic or electronic gadgets, yesterday's household goods are also far more satisfying to use. Old utensils have similar aesthetic advantages. Sets of saucepans, metal tea strainers, enamel colanders,

ladles, spatulas, rolling pins and sieves can be suspended from
a kitchen shelf where they are always close at hand. Keep your
eyes open for any other hardware that would add character to
your kitchen, from thermometers, tea trays and caddies to mops,
buckets and brooms.

If you want a traditional country kitchen, enhance the
reassuringly familiar look by adding an old refectory table, some
unpainted wooden cupboards, a few plain rush-seated chairs
or long benches and the most basic floor covering you can find:

heart of the home above

*Painter Charlotte Culot bought
her old range from a local village
in Provence. The charcoal-burning
stove keeps the winter chill at bay.*

bare boards, terracotta tiles or rush matting are perfect. Keep the look as uncomplicated and utilitarian as possible. Copper pans can be hung up for decoration (though any sign of damage means they are not safe to cook with), while old stove-top kettles, wooden utensils, salt-glazed storage jars and chunky earthenware pottery can be stowed on open shelves until needed.

Second-hand cooking ranges have long been highly prized for their warmth, good looks and efficiency, but prices tend to reflect the keen demand for machines in sound working condition, so always seek the advice of a qualified professional before having one installed, to make sure that you are spending your money wisely.

For a slightly more sophisticated kitchen, a different sort of junk sets the tone. Choose

whistling kettle **right**

A portable single gas burner is just the right size to boil up a tuneful cup of tea.

back to basics **below**

This simply furnished wooden barn deep in the Dutch countryside takes guests back to simpler times.

an old butler's sink and simple pieces of furniture painted in authentic shades of warm cream, pale blue and soft green. Tongue-and-groove wall panelling looks lovely when given the same treatment. Line shelves with rows of tins and enamelware, or display an assortment of patterned crockery on wall-mounted wooden plate racks or simple cup hooks – all will contribute more to the room's style and mood than their modest price-tag might suggest.

As well as being decorative, old tins can be restored to their original purpose and used to store anything from dried fruit to flour. Other groceries can be stored in old meat safes, wooden crates, baskets, galvanized buckets and even large preserving pans.

Cleaning materials should be kept out of sight beneath the sink, concealed by a curtain that can be simply made by gathering a piece of old fabric on a length of wire.

in the balance **above**

Traditional commercial scales have a reassuringly reliable quality.

little pitchers **below**

Jugs are indispensable around the kitchen for serving iced water or for holding flowers.

limed wood left

The woodwork in this kitchen has been 'aged' with white acrylic paint sanded smooth.

labelled up above

Any lettering on an object, especially if in a foreign language, adds to its charm.

old and new **left**

A quirky collection of junk baskets and containers adds character to modern kitchen equipment and units.

a unified whole **right**

An accumulation of interesting finds has been put together in this kitchen to create a room redolent of farmhouse living.

good service **below**

The best junk finds earn their keep by being functional as well as looking good.

display

This beautifully battered linen closet has been painted to match the monochrome bedroom.

bedrooms

Your bedroom should be more relaxed and comfortable than any other part of the house. Filling it with junk-shop finds will strike just the right balance between indulgence and simplicity; imagine a plain wrought-iron bed made up with white cotton sheets and covered with a downy quilt, and you'll appreciate the essence of this style.

overwrought

This ornate iron bed came from a Belgian flea market. The white linen was found closer to its Provençal home in the famous Isle sur la Sorgue market.

old linen **top**

Simple bed linen with just a

hint of decoration is the best

dressing for an ornate bed.

brassed off **above/right**

Inspect painted-metal

bedsteads carefully – you might

find brass hidden beneath.

field of dreams left

*Large furniture sales are the
best place to go if you want to
choose from a range of antique
beds in one place. But be
prepared to transport your
bulky purchase home if you do
succumb to temptation.*

Battered antique bedsteads appear in all the usual junk-lovers'
haunts, and each will set a slightly different mood and style for
your bedroom. Sometimes headboards are available together
with their bases, mattresses or footboards, sometimes without.
But don't pass over a beautiful find just because it's incomplete, as
separate bases and mattresses can easily be bought or made to
fit. Falling in love with the headboard itself is the most important
thing. Remember, too, that the most unusual junk-shop finds can
be adapted to make bed heads – gates, plank doors and carved
panels can be cut to size and fitted to a base, so keep your mind
open to such possibilities while you are engaged in your search.

dormitory right

*This pair of iron school beds
was left behind by a previous
owner of the house. You may
be able to find similar ones in
salvage yards – or watch out
for announcements in local
papers that a local school or
nursing home is closing down.*

well handled **below**

Don't be too precious about cleaning up your finds. Rusty handles and flaking paint add to the charm of old pieces.

gateway **right and opposite**

Be bold with bedroom furniture. Weathered wooden gates can make quirky headboards and footboards.

Simple metal-framed beds originally designed for dormitories or hospitals are perfect for children because they are so sturdy, while more decorative wrought-iron versions – singles or doubles – are good for guest rooms. Showier and more intricate designs – perhaps a lit bateau or a bed with brass knobs – might be worth reserving for the master bedroom where a hint of grandeur will be beautifully offset by the room's humblef elements.

A romantic four-poster bed is a rare junk-shop find, but you could make your own version using reclaimed or recycled timber supports and draping them with plain white muslin.

The bedroom is a good place to mix old with new. Combine the charm of an old bedstead with the comfort of a modern mattress, or

team a vintage cotton cover with a new duvet. When buying new pillows, bolsters and quilts, choose ones filled in the traditional manner with duck feathers or, better still, goose down.

Bedroom furniture can be as minimal or as decorative as you like. Near-empty rooms that contain just a bed make a dramatic statement and are somehow deeply appealing. But bear in mind that the peace and tranquillity of this sort of space will quickly be shattered by too much clutter, so avoid this look unless you are impeccably tidy, have very few possessions, or

have space for a separate dressing room. A less austere solution is to add a few pieces of junk furniture. Store clothes in a wooden wardrobe, as large as you have space for, a chest of drawers or a linen press, or alternatively on a commercial metal clothes rail bought from a wholesale supplier or picked up in a junk sale.

When looking for bedside tables, think beyond conventional cabinets and use small round metal café tables, wooden stools or metal seats to keep your water jug and night-time reading close at hand.

original features **left**

This bedroom is in a house that dates from 1520. The walls have been left virtually as they were found after 30 years of neglect when the present owners moved in.

travelling bed **right**

This 1860s travelling bed was discovered in an antiques shop in Honiton, Devon. It came with an array of baggage labels collected during its days of being shunted around on trains with an earlier owner.

bathrooms

Reclaimed antique bathroom fittings are highly appealing to junk shoppers. Cast-iron roll-top bathtubs with claw feet are far superior to flimsy modern acrylic versions. The same goes for old porcelain sinks set in metal stands, huge chrome daisy-head shower attachments and Victorian toilets with their original high-mounted cisterns. And a few small touches can make all the difference to existing plain white fittings: swap the taps/faucets for reconditioned originals, add some down-to-earth junk-style accessories, whitewash the walls – and all that remains for you to do is turn on the water, get into the tub, lie back and relax.

114

bathing in style right

This bathtub travelled on the top of a car from a Brussels flea market to its home in Provence. It now occupies pride of place in Charlotte Culot's bathroom. An old wooden rack found on a farm has become a quirky towel rail.

shattered glass left

A fragment of mirror perched on the taps is all that's needed.

safely stored

Bathrooms are ideal places for showing off all those wonderful pieces of china you've collected. A classic white jug will find a home anywhere while pretty plates are useful for holding small bathroom items.

Infinite variety is available to those who
are prepared to scour salvage yards and
specialist outlets at home and abroad in
pursuit of something unique. Stumbling
on an old bathtub used as a cattle trough
in the middle of a field is less likely to
happen these days, but you may still be
lucky. Re-enamelling is always possible if
your tub is otherwise in good shape.

Devotees of junk style don't mind
having a sink, bathtub and toilet that
don't match, and don't object to using a
garden table as a washstand, as long as
the spirit of casual simplicity reigns. So
combine styles and designs according to
what's available and what looks best.

Once you have established the look
of the room with its main fixtures and

fittings, try to keep everything else as simple and uncluttered as
possible. Bathrooms need a surprising amount of storage space in
order to maintain their clean lines. Pieces of furniture imported
from elsewhere in the house can all find a home here: store
toiletries in a spare kitchen cabinet, hang bathrobes on an unused
peg rail brought up from the pantry, or pile towels into an empty
blanket box from the bedroom.

Traditional-style items of bathroom furniture are as useful as
ever, so when out shopping keep your eyes open for old lockable
medicine chests, small mirrored cabinets and tile-backed
washstands. For authenticity's sake, combine them with a porcelain
or enamel pitcher-and-bowl set and piles of soft cotton hand-
towels. Other classic bathroom accessories, such as glass shelf
units, mirrors, tooth mugs, toothbrush holders, soap dishes and -

light and airy **above**

A charming basin has been
tucked into the eaves of this
Normandy barn. The mirror
has been unceremoniously
sliced to fit the space neatly.

chrome heated towel rails, also appear
from time to time in flea markets.
Otherwise, improvise with a piece of
driftwood as a bathroom shelf, a gold-
framed drawing-room mirror above the
sink, an old glass tumbler to hold the
toothbrushes, a floral-patterned china
saucer as a soap dish, or a basic wooden
trestle as a towel rail. Similarly, if you
can't find a bath mat made in the old-
fashioned way from duckboard slats or
cork, use a small hearth rug instead.

Flowers can give as much pleasure
in the bathroom as in any other room in
the house, so place a small vase on the
washstand or bathroom shelf, or hang up
a bunch of lavender to keep the air
fresh. Such small details will enhance the
sensual pleasure of your bathroom.

118

nautical sink **below**

*This seaside junk shop buy was
once owned by a sea captain.*

all at sea **left**

Ships from a London warehouse

introduce a sea-going theme.

salvage job **above**

A little restoration work can

revive an enamelled sink.

crossed wires

far left, top

Twisted metalwork
containers are ideal for
bathroom storage — excess
water will drain away.

soap stars

far left, below

Enamelware dishes
come in all shapes, even
shells. Lettering makes
them more collectable.

sinking feeling left

Look out for unusually
shaped basins. Industrial
designs are often
more interesting than
domestic versions.

reinvention above

This chunky ashtray
is far more suitably
employed holding blocks
of soap than for its
original purposes.

trough **above/right**

The unusually deep bath in
this elegant panelled bathroom
is actually a cattle trough that
was found abandoned in a
Lincolnshire field. The wooden
feet were made specially
to support it, and the
taps/faucets have been fitted
to the wall to avoid damaging
the trough itself.

ship ahoy **above**

White-painted walls and white

tiles maximize the light from an

old ship's lamp – a characterful

accent in a bathroom.

workrooms,
studies and studios

125

workstation

*Surround yourself with stylish
accessories while you work to
create an atmosphere
conducive to concentration.*

Whether you run a business from home or just need
somewhere peaceful to write letters, pay bills, pursue hobbies or
store papers, a workspace is essential. Filling your study with
modern office furniture would make it efficient, tidy and well
organized, but its dull uniformity and lack of character would
leave much to be desired. Turn instead to junk and you will be
able to create somewhere with style, flair and a distinctly human
touch. Even in the most minimalist environment, a few quirky and
characterful pieces of furniture will be inspirational. First, choose
a location. If you are lucky enough to have a whole room at your
disposal, it's relatively easy to create a business-like workspace –
there's also the advantage of being able to shut the door on
everything at the end of the day. For a rather less spacious office,
but one that can still accommodate a small writing table, use part
of a wide landing or the corner of a bedroom or dining room.

If you select your furniture and accessories with as much care
as you would take in choosing items for the rest of your home, a
workspace will not jar in the context of your other furnishings but
blend in seamlessly with the areas in which you live and relax.

First on your shopping list will be a work table. An old roll-top desk can be ideal, especially one with lots of built-in drawers, letter racks and pen holders. But this sort of piece can be expensive, and often a simple kitchen table or console will do just as well. If your studio is used for crafts or practical work, such as painting or sewing, a large wooden trestle – or even an old door resting on two low cupboards – will more than suffice.

A comfortable seat, ideally one that is adjustable and offers good back support, is your next priority. Why not look out for chairs that were originally intended for office use? It seems an appropriate form of recycling to return furniture like this to its original function. And by its very nature, good office furniture will have been ergonomically designed for comfort in use.

Find out when office clearances are taking place in your area, but also look out for older styles at sales and auctions, such as adjustable architect's chairs with low back supports and wooden swivel chairs on castors – they still look

126

window seat **left**

A small folding table used as an impromptu desk makes the most of the light that streams in through a dormer window.

space to spare **above**

This journalist's office is deliberately kept as spare as possible, with an old typewriter in place of a computer.

great and their classic clean lines work perfectly in a contemporary junk style environment.

You will need to devise some ingenious storage solutions to keep documents, books, stationery, materials and equipment in good order, especially in a small space. Many people also find that they work better in uncluttered surroundings. Shelving is essential – whether you use lengths of bare plank and some old bricks or find a cheap bookcase in a junk shop.

Office clearances are an excellent source of pieces such as solid wood filing cabinets, plain metal drawer units, large plan chests and old metal lockers. For smaller-scale organization, use an old vase as a pen pot, rattan baskets as in-trays, leather trunks for filing paperwork, and hat boxes for stowing any other odds and ends.

There's not much you can do to disguise the unattractive look of equipment such as printers and computers, but an old typewriter or a reconditioned Bakelite telephone will help redress the balance and prevent hi-tech styling taking over completely.

Adjustable anglepoise desk lamps, also reminiscent of another era, are still practical and stylish options for all kinds of close work.

conservatories
and greenhouses

A sense of the natural world, with its wonderful colours and scents, and all its graceful dust and decay, is the overwhelming atmosphere in a greenhouse. Carry an old wooden bench out here to work on – it can double up as a makeshift dining table in the cooler months when the garden is out of bounds. Gather old garden tools, either hanging them from hooks and nails or leaning them up in a corner ready for use. Along with the plants, these work-smoothed trugs, gardening gloves, shears, spades and forks are the only decoration your conservatory needs.

potted history

below left

Timeworn wood, terracotta, clay and painted brick give a potting shed traditional appeal.

inside out **below**

This wonderfully organized garden room is filled with an eclectic mixture of plants, ladders, trugs and straw hats.

129

under glass **above**

A flourishing potting shed can be a place for activity as well as for relaxation.

terracotta **left**

More attractive than any modern counterpart, old flowerpots proliferate at garage and yard sales.

old world **above/below**

A covered studio adjacent to a converted
barn is filled with weathered furniture and
the artist-owner's canvasses.

bench mark **right**

Redolent of traditional skills, even the
most ordinary workbench can become
an understated decorative feature.

living
outdoors

Any patch of garden, however small, can become an outdoor haven in fine weather. Even a narrow balcony or the smallest paved area beside the back door will provide room enough for a small marble-topped table and white-painted metal chairs where you can eat breakfast or lunch on a summer's day.

Furnish your outdoor space accordingly, making use of junk style in the same way as you do inside the house. Just as you can happily use garden furniture indoors, by the same token you can transfer furniture that was originally designed for the home to an outdoor setting. The effects of ageing, such a key part of

summer life **right**
A semi-covered area sheltered from the elements is used as a seasonal dining room.

al fresco **left/far right**
Take lunch in the shade of a leafy tree or set the table for dinner. Hurricane lamps will provide light as dusk falls.

the appeal of junk style, are
accelerated when furniture
is directly exposed to the
natural elements.

And if you've picked up
an old table and some chairs
at relatively little cost, you
are not going to be too upset
when the paint blisters or
lichen makes its home in the
cracks of bare wood. Even
fabrics can be left to take
their chances – deckchair
canvas allowed to bleach in
the sun until its gaudy stripes
have faded to shadows.

garden display **top row**

Outdoor ornamentation takes many forms, from the pleasingly practical to the purely decorative, such as a flag. Visible signs of decay are optional extras.

a dog's life **below left**

Even your animals can enjoy the benefits of junk style. This contented canine surveys outdoor activities from the comfort of a blanket-lined basket.

135

time for tea **below centre**

Outdoor furniture should not be too delicate – choose pieces that will withstand the odd shower. Their weathered look will add to the sense of informality.

day bed **below**

Piled with cushions and pillows to soften the hard metal, an ironwork lounger provides a quiet place to relax and enjoy the scenery.

abandoned in situ **above**

*A forgotten plough lies rusting in a field,
a reminder of a bygone age.*

back to nature **below/right**

*Lunch is served outside in a specially chosen part
of the orchard surrounding Yuri Kuper's house.
The tables and chairs are his own designs,
their wooden surfaces allowed to mellow with
age and a covering of lichen.*

One of greatest pleasures of outdoor living, and one of the most enjoyable ways of relaxing with friends, is dining in the open air. Choose a sheltered position for your garden table and chairs – this could be on the lawn, in a cobbled clearing at the bottom of the garden, or closer to the house on a terrace or veranda. So that you can enjoy alfresco meals in the heat of the midday sun, ensure there is some shade – an old parasol, a canopy of vines or a shady tree will all do the job.

Junk dining furniture made from metal, rattan, wicker or wood is ideal. If it is slightly faded, rusted or weather-worn to start with, so much the better. Either leave a wooden table top on show or throw over a simple checked cloth or an old white sheet, adding generously filled jugs of garden flowers to capture the lazy mood of high summer. Add plenty of

137

138

soft cushions covered in easy-going cotton if your chairs aren't as comfortable as they might be – you could make over-sized covers from an assortment of remnants and keep a spare set to wrap around your living-room cushions. Set the table with the same pieces you would use for indoor dining. None of your robust glass tumblers, flea-market china plates, worn linen napkins or odd pieces of cutlery is too precious to be transferred into the garden – and all are far nicer than the usual plastic knives and forks or paper plates and cups. To allow your guests to enjoy the occasion far into the evening, hang hurricane lamps and storm lanterns in the trees and light them as dusk falls. Cheaper and easier still are old jars with a plain white candle or night-light inside, protected from any stray breezes.

Life in the garden proves how versatile and easy-going junk style can be. Who would swap the ease with which possessions can be moved from house to garden and back again for the restrictions and tensions of conventional living?

sea view **above/right**

When you live this close to the sea, the beach becomes your garden, so use sympathetic materials such as reclaimed wood.

a breath of fresh air

Traditional wooden deckchairs
covered in unbleached canvas
allow visitors to enjoy the sea
breeze in comfort and style.

resources in the UK

*See websites for location
details and opening times.*

Architectural salvage

Andy Thornton
Victoria Mills
Halifax HX4 8AD
+ 44 (0)1422 376000
www.andythornton.com

Dicksons Architectural Salvage
www.architectural-
salvage.co.uk
+ 44 (0)191 387 5272

Dorset Reclamation
Cow Drove, Bere Regis
Dorset BH20 7JZ
www.dorsetreclamation.co.uk
+ 44 (0)1929 472200

LASSCo
+ 44 (0)20 7394 2100
www.lassco.co.uk

MASCo Salvage
Cirencester Road
Stroud GL6 8PE
www.mascosalvage.com
+ 44 (0)1285 760886

Walcot Reclamation
108 Walcot Street
Bath BA1 5BG
www.walcotarchitectural
salvage.co.uk
+ 44 (0)1225 469557

Wells Reclamation
Coxley, Wells BA5 1RQ
www.wellsreclamation.com
+ 44 (0)1749 677087

Furniture and accessories

After Noah
121 Upper Street
London N1 1QP
www.afternoah.com
+ 44 (0)20 7359 4281

Appley Hoare Antiques
9 Langton Street
London SW10 0JL
www.appleyhoare.com
+ 44 (0)20 7351 5206

Baileys
Whitecross Farm
Bridstow
Ross-on-Wye HR9 6JU
www.baileyshome.com
+ 44 (0)1989 563015

Bed Bazaar
The Old Station
Framlingham IP13 9EE
www.bedbazaar.co.uk
+ 44 (0)1728 723756

Castle Gibson Furniture
www.castlegibson.com
+ 44 (0)20 8211 8690

Cath Kidston
www.cathkidston.co.uk
+ 44 (0)1480 226199

The Conran Shop
www.conranshop.co.uk
0844 848 4000

The Curtain Agency
103 West Street
Farnham GU9 7EN
www.thecurtainagency.co.uk
+ 44 (0)1252 714711

Decorative Living
55 New King's Road
London SW6 4SE
www.decorativeliving.co.uk
+ 44 (0)20 7736 5623

Fern Avenue Antiques Centre
75–79 Fern Avenue
Newcastle upon Tyne
NE2 2RA
www.fernavenueantiques
centre.co.uk
+ 44 (0)191 209 4104

Josephine Ryan Antiques
www.josephineryanantiques.
co.uk
+ 44 (0)7973 336149

The Lacquer Chest
75 Kensington Church Street
London W8 4BG
www.lacquerchest.com
+ 44 (0)20 7937 1306

Lunn Antiques
86 New King's Road
London SW6 4LU
www.lunnantiques.co.uk
+ 44 (0)20 7736 4638

Mark Maynard Antiques
26 High Street
Tunbridge Wells TN1 1UX
markmaynard.co.uk
+ 44 (0)1892 617000

Petersham Nurseries
Richmond
Surrey TW10 7AG
www.petershamnurseries.com
+ 44 (0)20 8940 5230

Pimpernel & Partners
596 Kings Road
London SW6 2DX
www.pimpernelandpartners.
co.uk
+ 44 (0)20 7731 2448

Spencer Swaffer Antiques
30 High Street
Arundel BN18 9AB
www.spencerswaffer.com
+ 44 (0)1903 882132

Squint
178 Shoreditch High Street
London E1 6HU
www.squintlimited.com
+ 44 (0)20 7739 9275

Summerill & Bishop
www.summerillandbishop.com
+ 44 (0)20 7229 1377

Stiffkey Bathrooms
89 Upper St Giles Street
Norwich NR2 1AB
+ 44 (0)1603 627850
www.stiffkeybathrooms.com

Tobias and The Angel
68 White Hart Lane
London SW13 0PZ
www.tobiasandtheangel.com
+ 44 (0)20 8878 8902

Country and outdoor fairs

International Antiques and
Collectors' Fairs take place
regularly at Newark, Ardingly,
Shepton Mallet, Swinderby,
Newbury and Redbourn
www.iacf.co.uk
+ 44 (0)1636 702326

Penman Antiques Fairs take
place at Chester, Guildford,
Petersfield and London
www.penman-fairs.co.uk
+ 44 (0)1825 744074

For information on the many
other antiques fairs held
regularly around the UK, see
www.antiques-atlas.com

Antiques markets and flea markets

Alfie's Antique Market
13–25 Church Street
Marylebone
London NW8 8DT
alfiesantiques.com

Bermondsey Antiques Market
Bermondsey Square
London SE1 4QB
www.bermondseysquare.
co.uk/antiques.html

Brick Lane Market
London E1 6PU
www.visitbricklane.org

Camden Markets
London NW1
www.camdenlock.net

The Furniture Cave
533 Kings Road
London SW10 0TZ
www.furniturecave.co.uk

Greenwich Market
London SE10
www.greenwich-market.co.uk

Portobello Road Market
London W11 2QB
www.portobelloroad.co.uk

140

resources in the US

Many companies sell items online and have stores and outlets across the country. Check websites for details, including store locations and opening times.

Architectural salvage

Architectural Accents
2711 Piedmont Road NE
Atlanta, GA 30305
www.architecturalaccents.com
+ 1 404 266 8700

Architectural Paneling, Inc.
979 Third Avenue
New York, NY 10022
www.apaneling.com
+ 1 212 371 9632

Caravati's Inc.
104 East Second Street
Richmond, VA 23224
www.caravatis.com
+ 1 804 232 4175

Harrington Brass Works
www.harringtonbrassworks.
com
+ 1 201 818 1300

Salvage One Architectural
Elements
1840 W. Hubbard
Chicago, IL 60622
www.salvageone.com
+ 1 312 733 0098

Furniture and accessories

ABC Carpet & Home
www.abchome.com
+ 1 212 473 3000
(Manhattan store)

Altered Antiques
www.altered-antiques.com
+ 1 570 341 7668

Anthropologie
us.anthropologie.com
+ 1 800 309 2500
(toll free in the US)

Fishs Eddy
889 Broadway
New York, NY 10003
www.fishseddy.com
+ 1 212 420 2090

Knoll
www.knoll.com
+ 1 800 343 5665
(toll free in the US)

Ochre
www.ochre.net
+ 1 212 414 4332

Pottery Barn
www.potterybarn.com
+ 1 888 779 5176
(toll free in the US)

R 20th Century Design
82 Franklin Street
New York, NY 10013
www.r20thcentury.com
+ 1 212 343 7979

Restoration Hardware
www.restorationhardware.
com
+ 1 212 260 9479
(Manhattan store)

Ruby Beets Antiques
25 Washington Street
PO Box 1174
Sag Harbor, NY 11963
+ 1 631 899 3275

Flea markets

Several websites offer countrywide listings of flea markets. See, for example, www.greatfleamarket.com and fleaportal.com

The Antiques Garage/
West 25th Street Market/
Hell's Kitchen Flea Market
New York, NY 10001
www.hellskitchen
fleamarket.com

Brimfield Antique Show
Route 20, Brimfield,
MA 01010
www.brimfieldshow.com
+ 1 413 245 3436

Colorado Springs Flea Market
5225 East Platte Avenue
(Highway 24)
Colorado Springs, CO 80915
www.csfleamarket.com
+ 1 719 380 8599

Englishtown Auction Sales
90 Wilson Avenue
Englishtown, NJ 07726
www.englishtownauction.com
+ 1 732 446 9644

Flea Market at Eastern Market
Seventh Street, SE at Eastern
Market
Washington, DC 20003
www.easternmarket.net
+ 1 703 534 7612

Fort Lauderdale Swap Shop
3291 W. Sunrise Boulevard
Fort Lauderdale, FL 33311
www.floridaswapshop.com
+ 1 954 791 7927

French Market in New
Orleans
1008 North Peters Street
New Orleans, LA 70116
www.frenchmarket.org
+ 1 504 522 2621

Hartville Marketplace and
Flea Market
1289 Edison Street NW
Hartville, OH 44632
www.hartvillefleamarket.com
+ 1 330 877 9860

Kane County Flea Market
Rt. 64 and Randall Road
Saint Charles, IL 60174
www.kanecountyfleamarket.
com
+ 1 630 377 2252

Lakewood Antiques Market
1321 Atlanta Highway
Cumming, GA 30040
www.lakewoodantiques.com
+ 1 770 889 3400

Long Beach Antique Market
Long Beach Veterans Stadium
4901 E. Conant Street
Long Beach, CA 90808
www.longbeach
antiquemarket.com
+ 1 323 655 5703

Phoenix Park'n'Swap
3801 East Washington Street
Phoenix, AZ 85034
www.americanparknswap.com
+ 1 602 273 1250

Picc-a-dilly Flea Market
796 West 13th Street
Eugene, OR 97405
www.piccadillyflea.com
+ 1 541 683 5589

Redwood Swap Meet
3688 South Redwood Road
West Valley City, UT 84119
+ 1 801 973 6060

Rose Bowl Flea Market
100 Rose Bowl Drive
Pasadena, CA 91103
www.rgcshows.com
+ 1 323 560 7469

Renningers Market
740 Noble Street
Kutztown, PA 19530
+ 1 610 683 6848
www.renningers.com

Tennessee State Fairgrounds
Flea Market
625 Smith Avenue
Nashville, TN 37203
+ 1 615 862 5016

Traders Village
7979 N. Eldridge Road
Houston, TX 77041
www.tradersvillage.com
+ 1 281 890 5500

index

acknowledgements

Thanks to Tom Leighton for his kindness, good humour and for always taking beautiful pictures whatever the weather, and to Simon Whitmore, his assistant, for keeping us on the right road. Also to Larraine Shamwana for her consistent encouragement and great art direction – her huge contribution to pulling this project together creatively will not be forgotten. I couldn't have asked for a better team to travel and work with.

I am indebted to the owners of the wonderful houses I've been allowed to photograph, all of whom seemed to share the same spirit: garden antiques expert Peter Hone, garden designer Arne Maynard, Marilyn Phipps, interior designer Philip Hooper, artist Yuri Kuper, painter Charlotte Culot and lighting designer Alexis Aufray, designers Roxanne Beis and Jean-Bernard Navier, Netty Nauta, Caroline and Michael Breet, Aleid Rontgen and Annette Brederode, Glen Senk and Keith Johnson of Anthropologie, Jim and Pat Cole of Coming to America, and George Laaland at Woolloomooloo Restaurant. I'm grateful to the following shops for kindly allowing us to photograph their wonderful collections of second-hand furniture and accessories: Xavier Nicod, Potted Gardens, Ruby Beets and Fishs Eddy. I would also like to thank all my friends and colleagues who helped me to track them down, especially Polly and Mark Gilbey in London, Roxanne Beis and Amelie Thiodet in France, Nina Monfils in Holland and Andrea Raisfeld in New York.

Thanks to all at Ryland Peters & Small, especially Jacqui Small for giving me this great opportunity and my patient and long-suffering editor Sian Parkhouse. Alice Westgate should also not go unmentioned for all her hard work. Thanks also to my sister Caroline for her translations, to Fiona Craig McFeely and Jo Tyler for their help and to my agent, Fiona Lindsay.

On a personal front, thanks to my brilliant sons, George and Ralph, for taking my too frequent absences over the summer in such good humour and of course to Belinda for keeping things together at home. Above all, thanks to my wonderful husband, Martin, for everything.